SCHOLASTIC

Follow-the-Directions
Draw & Write Activities

Step-by-Step Directions and Writing Prompts That Guide Children to Draw Pictures and Write Stories About Them

BY KRISTIN GELLER

NEW YORK · TORONTO · LONDON · AUCKLAND · SYDNEY
MEXICO CITY · NEW DELHI · HONG KONG · BUENOS AIRES

Teaching *Resources*

For my first and best teachers,
my mom and dad,
Robert & Sarah Emrich

Cover and interior design by Holly Grundon
Cover and interior illustrations by Amanda Gulliver, except page 45 by Teresa Anderko

ISBN: 0-439-47122-2
Copyright © 2005 by Kristin Geller
Published by Scholastic Inc.
All rights reserved.
Printed in the U.S.A.

5 6 7 8 9 10   40   13 12 11 10 09 08

Contents

Introduction

Children love to draw pictures and then use their pictures as a starting place for their own creative stories. Drawing and storytelling provide wonderful outlets for children's rich imaginations. Even so, many children benefit from encouragement and guidance in both of these areas. The drawing activities and storytelling prompts in this book are designed to help children tap into their creativity as artists and writers. At the same time, they give children practice in following directions—a great way to prepare them for taking tests.

Each of the 35 reproducible activities in this book features simple, step-by-step directions for drawing a picture, followed by a writing prompt that encourages children to write about their picture. Drawing a picture is a highly motivating prewriting activity that helps children start formulating a story even before they begin writing. And because the writing prompts are open-ended, all students will be able to complete the activities with success.

The activities in this book show children how to draw a wide range of pictures that spark ideas for interesting stories and connect to favorite teaching themes, such as animals, transportation, and seasons. The drawing lessons also help children:

✳ learn to follow visual and written directions.

✳ build fine-motor skills.

✳ strengthen eye-hand coordination.

✳ develop near-point copying skills.

✳ gain confidence in their artistic abilities.

✳ learn basic shapes.

The appealing pages feature easy-to-read and easy-to-follow directions that allow children to complete the activities independently. The activities are designed for flexible use in the classroom or at home. Use them as the starting point for writing lessons, or place them in a center for independent work. Or have children complete the activities at the beginning of the day when they arrive in the classroom, after lunch, or while they are waiting for other students to complete an activity. The activity pages can also be sent home for instant and engaging homework.

Follow-the-Directions Draw & Write Activities connects to children's natural interests in drawing and telling stories and provides them with the support they need to let their imaginations soar!

How to Use This Book

The activities in this book can be used in any order to meet the needs of your students and the requirements of your curriculum. To introduce children to the concept of following visual and written directions, begin with the simpler, six-step activities, such as the hot air balloon on page 35. When students are ready for more of a challenge, progress to the eight-step activities, such as the seal on page 21. Look through the table of contents to find activities that connect to topics of study, such as insects, ocean creatures, or modes of transportation. The activities can be used in a variety of ways, such as:

❋ fiction and nonfiction writing lessons.

❋ extension activities for literature response.

❋ classroom displays and bulletin boards.

❋ thematic units.

❋ genre studies.

❋ homework.

❋ learning centers.

❋ collaborative class books.

Each step-by-step drawing activity is accompanied by an open-ended writing prompt that jump-starts the writing process. The prompts encourage students to write both fiction and nonfiction pieces in variety of genres, such as personal narrative, expository writing, humorous fiction, and science fiction. The activity pages feature three different kinds of writing prompts:

Story Starters   These prompts feature three different story beginnings for students to choose from, such as narrating a personal experience, writing a creative story, and writing a factual story.

Story Outlines   These prompts provide students with a story beginning, followed by the sequence words *first*, *next*, *then*, and *last*. This format offers children a structure with which to organize their writing sequentially. It also helps them develop an awareness that stories have a beginning, middle, and ending.

Question Starters   These prompts are in the form of questions designed to spark ideas for children's writing. By answering the questions, students will develop ideas and details for their writing. This format is helpful in teaching students about descriptive writing and elaboration.

On pages 42–47, you'll find reproducible stationery pages on which children can draw their pictures and write their stories. If students need an extra page for their writing, provide them with a photocopy of the lined paper on page 48.

Once you have selected an activity, make a copy of the page for each student. Make copies of a stationery page as well. Before having children complete the activities independently, model for them how to use one or two activities. Give each student a copy of the activity page and explain that the activity involves two parts: following the directions to draw a picture, and then using the writing prompt(s) to write a story about the picture.

Together, review the step-by-step drawing directions. On chart paper or the chalkboard, show students how to follow the drawing steps. Give students a copy of the stationery page and invite them to follow the steps to draw the picture in the frame. Then model for them how to choose a writing prompt and write a story about the picture.

To help students generate ideas for their stories, encourage them to activate prior knowledge about the topic and help them relate those experiences to the writing prompt. You might begin the activity by reading aloud an engaging book that connects to the topic. Here's an example of a lesson in which I introduce the fish activity on page 9. I begin by reading aloud *Rainbow Fish,* by Marcus Pfister.

Teacher: Boys and girls, today we read *Rainbow Fish,* by Marcus Pfister. This story was about a beautiful fish that learned how to share. The author and illustrator did a remarkable job of matching the pictures to the story. What did the story and pictures make you think of?
(Students provide various responses.)

Teacher: This book made me want to write and illustrate my own story about a fish. Today I am going to use step-by-step drawing directions to help me draw my pictures. First, I look at the drawings, and then I read the directions. Let's look at them together on the page. These directions show me how to draw a fish.

I'll start with the first step: Draw 2 lines for the mouth. [I draw the mouth on chart paper.] Then I follow the next step. [I model each of the steps in the same way.] When I have finished drawing, I'll color the fish and decorate it any way I choose. Do you have any suggestions?
(Students provide various responses.)

Teacher: Next, I'm going to write a story about my fish. To help me begin my story, I'm going to use one of the Story Starters at the bottom of the page. [I read aloud the three Story Starters.] Which one would you choose?
(Students provide various responses.)

Teacher: I'll use the first one, because it reminds me of a time I went swimming. Let me tell my story before I write it. *One sunny day, I was swimming in a pond when I saw a tiny fish. It was a beautiful yellow fish with shiny, silvery scales on it. A boy who was swimming near me started to splash the fish. The fish got so scared that it quickly swam away. I hope that little fish got home safely!*

Now I'll write my story. When I write, I need to remember to use my sentence skills. What are some of the sentence skills we have been studying?
(Students provide various responses.)

Teacher: Those are all good examples. I'll put an uppercase letter at the beginning of each sentence, use periods at the end of each sentence, and leave spaces in between each word. When I remember to use my sentence skills, other people will be able to read my story and enjoy it. [I model writing the story and read it aloud.]

I hope the activities in this book spark many wonderful ideas for imaginative stories and encourage students to gain confidence in their skills as artists and writers. Enjoy drawing, writing, and sharing stories together!

Name _____ **Date** _____

Draw It!

Follow the directions to draw a bee.
Draw your picture on the next page.

| **1** Draw a small circle for the head. | **2** Draw an oval for the body.  | **3** Draw 2 circles for the top wings. 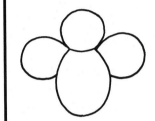 | **4** Draw 2 circles for the bottom wings. 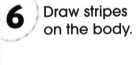 |
| **5** Draw a triangle for the stinger.  | **6** Draw stripes on the body.  | **7** Draw 2 curved lines for antennae. 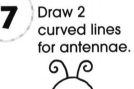 | **8** Draw a face.  |

Write About It!

Choose a Story Starter. Then write about your picture on the next page.

✳ Once a little bumblebee got lost on his way to the hive. He . . .

✳ There's a lot to know about bees. They . . .

✳ Hello! I'm a busy bee. But I have time to tell you . . .

Follow-the-Directions Draw & Write Activities   Scholastic Teaching Resources

Name _____   **Date** _____

Draw It!

Follow the directions to draw a crab.
Draw your picture on the next page.

1 Draw an oval for the body.

2 Draw 2 small squares with circles on top.

3 Draw 2 rectangles for legs.

4 Draw pointed shapes for claws.

5 Draw curved lines for legs (4 on each side).

6 Draw eyes and a curved line for the mouth.

Write About It!

Choose a Story Starter. Then write about your picture on the next page.

* One day at the beach, I saw a crab crawling . . .

* At the bottom of the ocean lived a tiny crab named . . .

* Have you ever seen a hermit crab? They . . .

Follow-the-Directions Draw & Write Activities   Scholastic Teaching Resources

Name _____   **Date** _____

Draw It!

Follow the directions to draw a fish.
Draw your picture on the next page.

1 Draw 2 lines for the mouth.	**2** Draw a curved line for the top of the body.	**3** Draw a curved line for the bottom of the body.	**4** Draw 2 ovals for the tail.
5 Draw a curved line for the head. 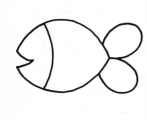	**6** Draw curved lines for fins. 	**7** Draw wiggly lines for gills. 	**8** Draw bubbles and an eye. 

Write About It!

Choose a Story Starter. Then write about your picture on the next page.

✳ One sunny day, I was swimming when . . .

✳ Last summer I went fishing with . . .

✳ Swim, swim, swim. I'm a fish! Did you know . . . ?

Name _____   **Date** _____

Draw It!

Follow the directions to draw a football.
Draw your picture on the next page.

1 Draw a curved line for the top of the football.

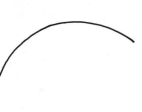

2 Draw a curved line for the bottom of the football.

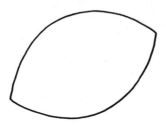

3 Draw 2 lines on one end.

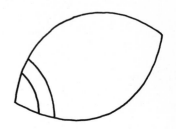

4 Draw 2 lines on the other end.

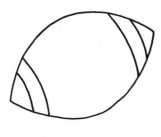

5 Draw an oval in the center.

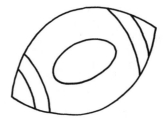

6 Draw 4 lines for the laces.

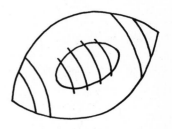

Write About It!

Choose a Story Starter. Then write about your picture on the next page.

✳ My favorite football team . . .

✳ Wow! I couldn't believe how far I threw the football. It . . .

✳ Football is a fun sport! To play the game . . .

Follow-the-Directions Draw & Write Activities   Scholastic Teaching Resources

Draw It!

Follow the directions to draw an ice cream cone. Draw your picture on the next page.

1 Draw a half circle for the top of the scoop.

2 Draw curved lines for the bottom of the scoop.

3 Draw 2 lines for the cone.

4 Draw crisscross lines on the cone.

5 Draw dots for sprinkles.

6 Draw a circle and line for a cherry.

Write About It!

Choose a Story Starter. Then write about your picture on the next page.

✳ One hot summer day, I was eating an ice cream cone when . . .

✳ If I could invent a flavor of ice cream, I would . . .

✳ What would you do with the world's tallest ice cream cone? I would . . .

Draw It!

Follow the directions to draw a ladybug.
Draw your picture on the next page.

1 Draw 2 small circles with dots for eyes.	**2** Draw a curved line for the head.

3 Draw a large half circle for the body.

4 Draw a line across the bottom.

5 Draw 6 short lines for legs.

6 Draw curved lines for antennae and a mouth.

7 Draw circles for spots.

8 Color the spots black.

Write About It!

Choose a Story Starter. Then write about your picture on the next page.

※ A little ladybug landed on . . .

※ There are lots of different kinds of bugs . . .

※ Once I saw a ladybug crawling on a . . .

Draw It!

Follow the directions to draw a lion.
Draw your picture on the next page.

1 Draw a small triangle for the nose.	**2** Draw 2 circles touching the triangle.	**3** Draw a short curved line for the tongue.	**4** Draw a long curved line for the head.
5 Draw 2 small circles for ears.	**6** Draw 2 small circles with dots inside for eyes.	**7** Draw curved lines for the mane.	**8** Draw short lines for whiskers.

Write About It!

Choose a Story Starter. Then write about your picture on the next page.

✳ A large, lazy lion was . . .

✳ Did you know that lions can . . . ?

✳ A pride of lions was walking across . . .

Follow-the-Directions Draw & Write Activities   Scholastic Teaching Resources

Name _____ **Date** _____

Draw It!

Follow the directions to draw a monkey.
Draw your picture on the next page.

1 Draw 2 curved lines for the top of the head.

2 Draw 2 half circles for ears.

3 Draw a curved line for the bottom of the head.

4 Draw 2 ovals for the body.

5 Draw curved lines for arms and legs.

6 Draw round shapes for fingers and toes.

7 Draw a long, curved tail.

8 Draw a face.

Write About It!

Choose a Story Starter. Then write about your picture on the next page.

✳ I'm a monkey! Yesterday I did something funny. I . . .

✳ One day, I was walking through the jungle when . . .

✳ A little monkey was lost in the jungle. She climbed . . .

Follow-the-Directions Draw & Write Activities   Scholastic Teaching Resources

Name _____ **Date** _____

Draw It!

Follow the directions to draw an octopus.
Draw your picture on the next page.

1 Draw a curved line for the head.

2 On one side, draw 3 curved shapes for arms.

3 On the other side, draw 3 more curved shapes.

4 Draw 2 curved shapes in the middle.

5 Draw eyes and a mouth.

6 Draw wavy lines for water.

Choose a Story Starter. Then write about your picture on the next page.

Write About It!

✳ If I were an octopus, I would use my arms to . . .

✳ A young octopus wanted to learn how to juggle. First, . . .

✳ Have you ever wondered why an octopus . . . ?

Draw It!

Follow the directions to draw a planet.
Draw your picture on the next page.

1 Draw a large circle for the planet Saturn.

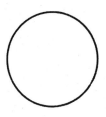

2 Draw a curved line for the ring.

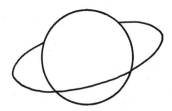

3 Draw another line for the ring.

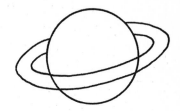

4 Color the ring.

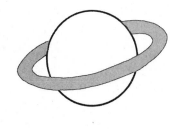

5 Draw lines across the planet.

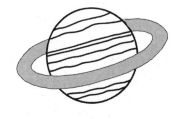

6 Draw details for outer space.

Write About It!

Choose a Story Starter. Then write about your picture on the next page.

✳ I am an astronaut. I traveled on a spaceship to . . .

✳ Saturn is an interesting planet. Did you know . . . ?

✳ Yesterday a friendly alien landed on the playground . . .

Follow-the-Directions Draw & Write Activities   Scholastic Teaching Resources

Draw It!

Follow the directions to draw a police car.
Draw your picture on the next page.

| **1** Draw a line with 2 circles for the wheels. | **2** Draw small rectangles for the bumpers. | **3** Draw a short curved line in the front. | **4** Draw a long curved line in the back. |
| **5** Draw small shapes for windows. | **6** Draw small circles for hubcaps and a headlight. | **7** Draw a half circle with lines for the light. | **8** Write the word POLICE. |

Write About It!

Choose a Story Starter. Then write about your
picture on the next page.

✳ If I interviewed a police officer, I would ask . . .

✳ A police car drove down the street and . . .

✳ Police officers are important because . . .

Draw It!

Follow the directions to draw a rainbow. Draw your picture on the next page.

1 On the left, draw curved lines for a cloud.	**2** Draw another cloud on the right.	**3** Draw a curved purple stripe.	**4** Draw a curved blue stripe.
5 Draw a curved green stripe.	**6** Draw a curved yellow stripe.	**7** Draw a curved orange stripe.	**8** Draw a curved red stripe.

Write About It!

Choose a Story Starter. Then write about your picture on the next page.

✳ A beautiful rainbow appeared in the . . .

✳ I followed a leprechaun to the end of a rainbow and . . .

✳ Did you know that rainbows . . . ?

Follow-the-Directions Draw & Write Activities   Scholastic Teaching Resources

Draw It!

Follow the directions to draw a robot.
Draw your picture on the next page.

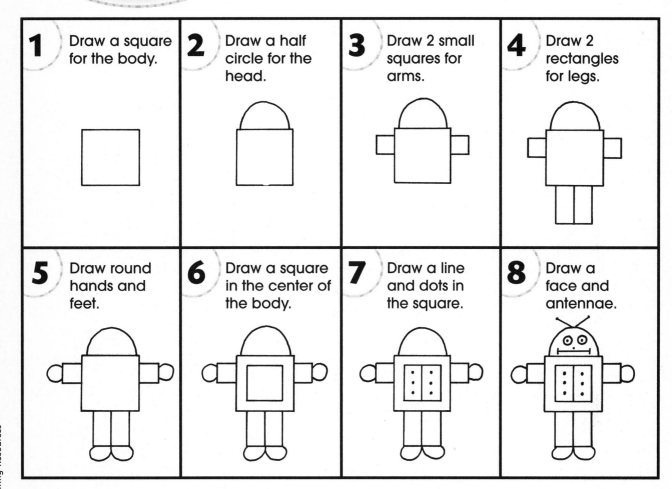

1 Draw a square for the body.

2 Draw a half circle for the head.

3 Draw 2 small squares for arms.

4 Draw 2 rectangles for legs.

5 Draw round hands and feet.

6 Draw a square in the center of the body.

7 Draw a line and dots in the square.

8 Draw a face and antennae.

Write About It!

Choose a Story Starter. Then write about your picture on the next page.

✻ I invented a robot! It helps me . . .

✻ A robot came to live with . . .

✻ Hello. I am a robot. I can . . .

Name _____ **Date** _____

Draw It!

Follow the directions to draw a sailboat.
Draw your picture on the next page.

1 Draw a half circle for the bottom of the boat.

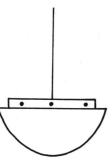

2 Draw a rectangle on top.

3 Draw dots for windows.

4 Draw a line for the mast.

5 Draw 2 triangles for the sails.

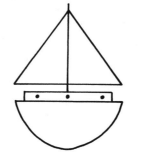

6 Draw wavy lines for water.

Write About It!

Choose a Story Starter. Then write about your picture on the next page.

✳ One windy day, a big sailboat . . .

✳ After our long journey, we finally spotted land! I . . .

✳ We raised the sails and were ready to . . .

Follow-the-Directions Draw & Write Activities · Scholastic Teaching Resources

Draw It!

Follow the directions to draw a seal.
Draw your picture on the next page.

1 Draw a curved line for the head.

2 Draw an oval for the snout.

3 Draw curved lines for the flippers.

4 Draw 2 curved lines for the body.

5 Draw 2 curved shapes for the tail.

6 Draw 2 circles with dots for eyes.

7 Draw a nose, mouth, and whiskers.

8 Draw lines on the flippers and tail.

Write About It!

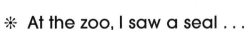

Choose a Story Starter. Then write about your picture on the next page.

✳ At the zoo, I saw a seal . . .

✳ Welcome to the icy waters of the Arctic Ocean. I'm a seal and I . . .

✳ Seals are amazing creatures! Did you know . . . ?

Name _____   **Date** _____

Draw It!

Follow the directions to draw a snail.
Draw your picture on the next page.

1 Draw a circle for the head.	**2** Draw a curved line for the body.	**3** Starting at the head, draw a large spiral for the shell.
4 Draw a triangle for the tail.	**5** Draw 2 small rectangles with circles on top.	**6** Draw a face.

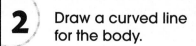

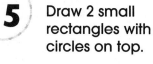

Write About It!

Choose a Story Starter. Then write about your picture on the next page.

✳ Once I saw a snail with a strange shell. It . . .

✳ A sleepy snail slowly crawled . . .

✳ Have you ever wondered why snails . . . ?

Follow-the-Directions Draw & Write Activities   Scholastic Teaching Resources

Name _____   **Date** _____

Draw It!

Follow the directions to draw a valentine.
Draw your picture on the next page.

1 Draw a curved line for half of the heart.	**2** Draw a curved line to finish the heart.	**3** Draw 2 diagonal lines on each side.

4 Draw a triangle for the tip of the arrow.	**5** Draw a triangle for the bottom of the arrow.	**6** Write the word LOVE inside the heart.
		LOVE

Write About It!

Choose a Story Starter. Then write about your picture on the next page.

✳ My favorite thing about Valentine's Day is . . .

✳ On Valentine's Day, I opened my mailbox and saw . . .

✳ I made a special Valentine's Day card for . . .

Name _____ **Date** _____

Draw It!

Follow the directions to draw a fire truck.
Draw your picture on the next page.

1 Draw a line with 2 circles for the wheels.

2 Draw a square for the front of the truck.

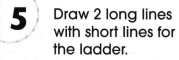

3 Draw a rectangle for the back of the truck.

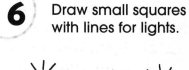

4 Draw a square for the window.

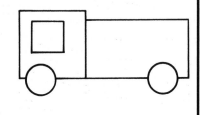

5 Draw 2 long lines with short lines for the ladder.

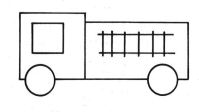

6 Draw small squares with lines for lights.

Write About It!

Follow the outline to write about your picture.
Write your story on the next page.

A fire truck went zooming down the street! First, it . . .

Next, . . .

Then, . . .

Last, . . .

Scholastic Teaching Resources

Follow-the-Directions Draw & Write Activities

Draw It!

Follow the directions to draw a flower.
Draw your picture on the next page.

1 Draw a small circle for the center of the flower.

2 Draw 5 small circles for petals.

3 Draw 2 lines for the stem.

4 Draw a thin rectangle for the top of the flowerpot.

5 Draw 3 lines for the bottom of the flowerpot.

6 Draw 2 spiral lines for leaves.

Follow the outline to write about your picture.
Write your story on the next page.

Write About It!

I planted a flower. First, I . . .

Next, . . .

Then, . . .

Last, . . .

Follow-the-Directions Draw & Write Activities   Scholastic Teaching Resources

Draw It!

Follow the directions to draw party balloons.
Draw your picture on the next page.

1 Draw an oval for a balloon.	**2** Draw another oval. 	**3** Draw small trapezoids at the bottom of each oval. 	**4** Draw small triangles in the ovals. 
5 Draw wavy lines for string. 	**6** Draw small squares for confetti. 	**7** Draw curly lines for more confetti. 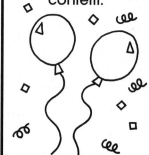	**8** Draw dots for even more confetti! 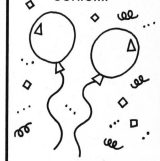

Write About It!

Follow the outline to write about your picture.
Write your story on the next page.

We had fun at the party. First, we . . .

Next, . . .

Then, . . .

Last, . . .

Follow-the-Directions Draw & Write Activities   Scholastic Teaching Resources

Draw It!

Follow the directions to draw a rabbit.
Draw your picture on the next page.

1 Draw a circle for the head.	
2 Draw 2 tall curved shapes for ears.	
3 Starting at the head, draw a curved line that spirals in. 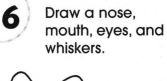	
4 Draw 2 curved lines for paws. 	
5 Draw a cloud shape for the tail. 	
6 Draw a nose, mouth, eyes, and whiskers. 	

Follow the outline to write about your picture.
Write your story on the next page.

Write About It!

I saw a rabbit hopping through my garden! First, it . . .

Next, . . .

Then, . . .

Last, . . .

Name _____ **Date** _____

Draw It!

Follow the directions to draw a sun.
Draw your picture on the next page.

1 Draw a large circle for the sun. 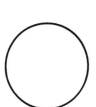	**2** Draw curved lines all around the sun. 	**3** Draw a line with 2 half circles for sunglasses. 
4 Color the sunglasses. 	**5** Draw curved lines for a nose and mouth. 	**6** Draw lines for rays. 

Write About It!

Follow the outline to write about your picture.
Write your story on the next page.

On sunny days, I like to play outside. First, I . . .

Next, . . .

Then, . . .

Last, . . .

Follow-the-Directions Draw & Write Activities   Scholastic Teaching Resources

Draw It!

Follow the directions to draw an umbrella.
Draw your picture on the next page.

1 Draw a large curved line for the top of the umbrella.

2 Draw smaller curved lines for the bottom of the umbrella.

3 Draw a straight line with a curve at the bottom.

4 Draw another straight line with a curve.

5 Draw lines on the umbrella.

6 Draw raindrops.

Write About It!

Follow the outline to write about your picture.
Write your story on the next page.

Once I was outside on a rainy day. First, I . . .

Next, . . .

Then, . . .

Last, . . .

Name _____ **Date** _____

Draw It!

Follow the directions to draw a bird.
Draw your picture on the next page.

1 Draw an oval for the body. 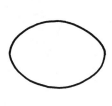	**2** Draw a circle for the head. 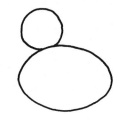
3 Draw a triangle for the beak. 	**4** Draw a shape with 3 bumps for the wing. 
5 Draw a shape with 3 bumps for the tail. 	**6** Draw lines for the legs and feet. 
7 Draw a circle for the eye. 	**8** Draw a dot inside the eye. 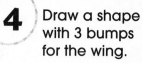

Write About It!

Answer the questions about your picture.
Use the answers to write a story on the next page.

✴ What is unusual about your bird?

✴ Where is the bird going?

✴ What will it do when it arrives?

Follow-the-Directions Draw & Write Activities   Scholastic Teaching Resources

Name _____ **Date** _____

Draw It!

Follow the directions to draw a castle.
Draw your picture on the next page.

1 Draw a large rectangle for the castle.

2 Draw 2 squares for towers.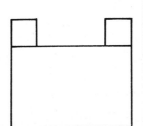

3 Draw a rectangle for a tall tower.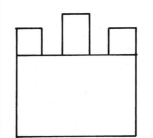

4 Draw triangles for the tops of the towers.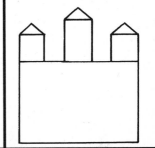

5 Draw a curved line for the door.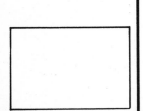

6 Draw squares for windows.

7 Draw details in the windows and door.

8 Draw 3 triangles for flags.

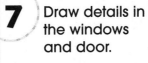

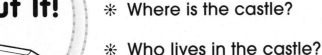

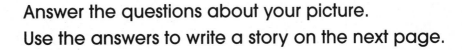

Write About It!

Answer the questions about your picture.
Use the answers to write a story on the next page.

✳ Where is the castle?

✳ Who lives in the castle?

✳ What adventures happened there?

Name _____   **Date** _____

Draw It!

Follow the directions to draw a clown.
Draw your picture on the next page.

1 Draw a triangle for the hat.	**2** Draw a small circle for a pom-pom.	**3** Draw 2 cloud shapes for hair.	**4** Draw a curved line for the chin.

5 Draw curved lines for the collar.	**6** Draw circles with dots for eyes.	**7** Draw a nose and mouth.	**8** Draw 2 lines for the body.

Answer the questions about your picture.
Use the answers to start a story on the next page.

Write About It!

✳ What is your clown's name?

✳ What special talents does the clown have?

✳ What happened to the clown at the circus?

Follow-the-Directions Draw & Write Activities · Scholastic Teaching Resources

Draw It!

Follow the directions to draw a gift.
Draw your picture on the next page.

1 Draw a large rectangle for the gift box.

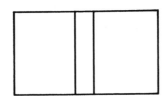

2 Draw 2 lines for the ribbon.

3 Draw a trapezoid for the bow.

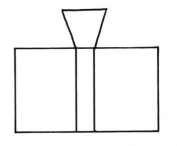

4 Draw 2 triangles to finish the bow.

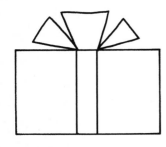

5 Draw lines in the bow for texture.

6 Draw a pattern with dots and circles.

Write About It!

Answer the questions about your picture.
Use the answers to write a story on the next page.

✴ Who is the gift for?

✴ Who is the gift from?

✴ What is special about this gift?

Draw It!

Follow the directions to draw a giraffe.
Draw your picture on the next page.

1 Draw a zigzag line with 2 circles for horns.	**2** Draw pointed lines for ears.	**3** Draw a curved line for the head.	**4** Draw 2 uneven lines for the neck.
5 Draw a curved line for the body.	**6** Draw a long line with short lines for the tail.	**7** Draw eyes, nostrils, and a mouth.	**8** Draw spirals for spots.

Write About It!

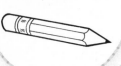

Answer the questions about your picture.
Use the answers to write a story on the next page.

✳ What is your giraffe's name?

✳ What is the giraffe's favorite activity?

✳ What can the giraffe do with its long neck?

Draw It!

Follow the directions to draw a hot air balloon.
Draw your picture on the next page.

 1 Draw a circle for the balloon.

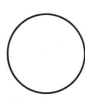 **2** Draw a square for the basket.

 **3** Draw 2 curved lines to connect the balloon and basket.

 **4** Draw 2 curved lines on the balloon.

 **5** Draw 2 more curved lines on the balloon.

 **6** Draw crisscross lines on the basket.

Answer the questions about your picture.
Use the answers to start a story on the next page.

Write About It!

* Who will ride in the hot air balloon?

* Where will the balloon go?

* What is it like to ride in the balloon?

Draw It!

Follow the directions to draw a monster.
Draw your picture on the next page.

1 Draw 2 ovals with dots for eyes.

2 Draw a curved line for the top of the mouth.

3 Draw a curved line for the bottom of the mouth.

4 Draw 2 ovals for feet.

5 Draw zigzag lines on one side.

6 Draw zigzag lines on the other side.

7 Draw lines for teeth.

8 Draw wiggly lines.

Write About It!

Answer the questions about your picture.
Use the answers to write a story on the next page.

✳ What is your monster's name?

✳ What does the monster like to eat?

✳ What adventure did the monster have?

Name _____ **Date** _____

Follow the directions to draw an owl.
Draw your picture on the next page.

1 Draw a circle for the head.

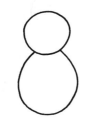

2 Draw a large oval for the body.

3 Draw 2 curved lines with bumps for wings.

4 Draw small ovals for the talons (claws).

5 Draw 2 circles with dots for eyes.

6 Draw 3 small triangles on the head.

7 Draw lines for texture.

8 Draw a branch with small leaves.

Write About It!

Answer the questions about your picture.
Use the answers to start a story on the next page.

✳ When did you see the owl?

✳ Where did you see the owl?

✳ What did the owl look like?

Name _____ **Date** _____

Draw It!

Follow the directions to draw a pumpkin.
Draw your picture on the next page.

1 Draw an oval.

2 Draw a curved line on each side of the oval.

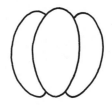

3 Draw another curved line on each side.

4 Draw a trapezoid for the stem.

5 Draw a curved shape for a leaf.

6 Draw a curly line for the vine.

Write About It!

Answer the questions about your picture.
Use the answers to write a story on the next page.

✳ Is there anything special about your pumpkin?

✳ Who picked the pumpkin?

✳ What happened to the pumpkin after it was picked?

Follow-the-Directions Draw & Write Activities   Scholastic Teaching Resources

Name _____ **Date** _____

Draw It!

Follow the directions to draw a snake.
Draw your picture on the next page.

1 Draw 2 ovals.

2 Draw a curved line for the head.

3 Draw a long wavy line for the body.

4 Draw another long wavy line below it.

5 Draw a mouth, tongue, and eyes.

6 Draw a pattern with lines and dots.

Write About It!

Answer the questions about your picture.
Use the answers to start a story on the next page.

✳ What is your snake's name?

✳ Where does the snake live?

✳ What is the snake's favorite activity?

Name _____   **Date** _____

Draw It!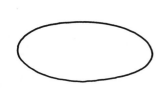

Follow the directions to draw a submarine.
Draw your picture on the next page.

1 Draw a large flat oval. 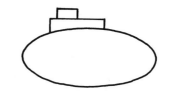	**2** Draw 2 thin rectangles on top of the oval. 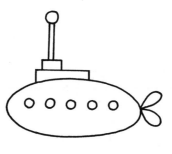	**3** Draw 2 lines with a circle on top for the periscope. 
4 Draw circles for windows. 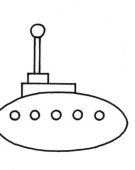	**5** Draw 2 ovals for the rudder.	**6** Draw wavy lines for water. 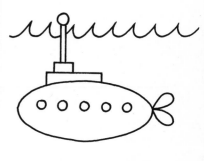

Write About It!

Answer the questions about your picture.
Use the answers to start a story on the next page.

✳ Who is inside the submarine?

✳ What are they doing?

✳ Where are they going?

Follow-the-Directions Draw & Write Activities   Scholastic Teaching Resources

Name _____   Date _____

Follow the directions to draw a train.
Draw your picture on the next page.

1 Draw a rectangle.

2 Draw 3 circles for wheels.

3 Draw lines to connect the wheels.

4 Draw a triangle with lines for the cowcatcher.

5 Draw a square with a square inside.

6 Draw a thin rectangle for the roof.

7 Draw a trapezoid for the smokestack.

8 Draw cloud shapes for smoke.

Write About It!

Answer the questions about your picture.
Use the answers to start a story on the next page.

✴ Who will ride on the train?

✴ What is the train carrying?

✴ Where is the train going?

Name _____ **Date** _____

_____

_____

_____

_____

_____

_____

_____

Name _____ **Date** _____

Name _____ **Date** _____

_____

_____

_____

_____

_____

_____

_____

Name _____ **Date** _____

Name _____   **Date** _____

_____

_____

_____

_____

Name _____   **Date** _____

_____

_____

_____

_____

_____

_____

Name _____   **Date** _____

_____

_____

_____

_____

_____

_____

_____

_____

_____